LIGHT

This book belongs to

Wonder House

THE GREEN TREES AND
THE SKY THAT IS BLUE

CAN YOU SEE THE COLORS OF THE
RAINBOW TOO?

A FORM OF ENERGY
THAT TRAVELS FAST

IT'S LIGHT THAT HELPS US
TO SEE ALL THAT WE PASS

SUN, STARS, FLASHLIGHT
AND FIREFLIES

ARE SOURCES OF LIGHT
FOR OUR EYES!

THE WORLD IS A BRIGHT PLACE
WITH LIGHT

WHAT WOULD WE SEE
WITHOUT LIGHT?

NOTHING AT ALL,
THAT'S RIGHT!

WHAT'S THAT??
IT'S SO DARK HERE! I CANNOT SEE ANYTHING.
LET ME TURN ON THE LIGHT.
OH! IT'S MY TEDDY.
WHAT IS LIGHT?
LIGHT IS A KIND OF ENERGY THAT WE SEE.
IT HELPS PLANTS TO MAKE FOOD
IT POWERS SOME OF THE THINGS WE USE
LIGHT GIVES US WARMTH
WITHOUT LIGHT WE WOULD NOT BE ABLE TO SEE...
THE MOON IN THE NIGHT SKY
THE COLORS OF THE RAINBOW
THE SUNSET
OR THE WAY AROUND
LIFE CANNOT EXIST ON EARTH WITHOUT LIGHT.

LIGHT- A FORM OF ENERGY

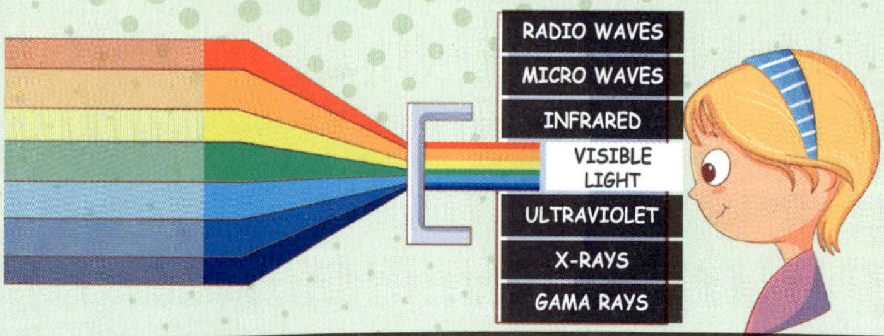

INFRARED AND ULTRAVIOLET RAYS ARE ALSO A PART OF LIGHT BUT WE CANNOT SEE THEM.

THE LIGHT WE SEE EVERY DAY IS CALLED VISIBLE LIGHT. IT IS A SMALL PORTION OF THE ELECTROMAGNETIC SPECTRUM, A MIXTURE OF ALL WAVELENGTHS OF THE VISIBLE SPECTRUM.

VISIBLE LIGHT IS ALSO CALLED WHITE LIGHT.
THE ELECTROMAGNETIC SPECTRUM INCLUDES OTHER RADIATIONS TOO. THESE ARE:

WAVELENGTH

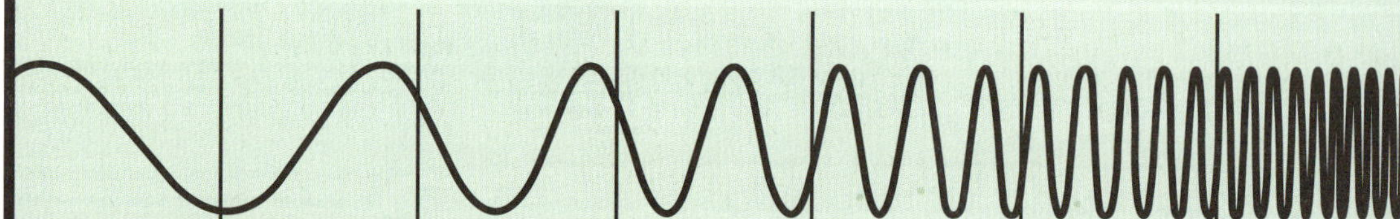

RADIO	MICROWAVES	INFRARED	VISIBLE LIGHT	ULTRAVIOLET	X-RAYS	GAMMA RAYS
		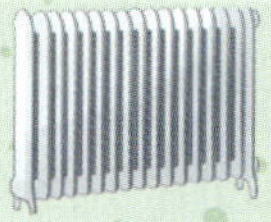			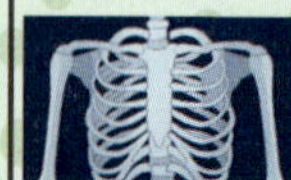	
USED TO BROADCAST ON RADIO AND TELEVISION	USED IN COOKING, RADAR, TELEPHONE AND OTHER SIGNALS	TRANSMITS HEAT FROM SUN, FIRES, RADIATORS	MAKES THINGS SEEN OR VISIBLE	ABSORBED BY THE SKIN, USED IN FLUORESCENT TUBES	USED TO SEE INSIDE THE BODY AND OBJECTS	USED IN MEDICINE FOR KILLING CANCER CELLS

FORMS OF LIGHT
LIGHT EXISTS IN TWO DIFFERENT FORMS. ONE FORM IS TINY PARTICLES CALLED PHOTONS AND THE OTHER, WAVES.
LIGHT SOURCE
PARTICLES CALLED PHOTONS
WAVES
THE WAVES OF LIGHT HAVE PEAKS AND VALLEYS. THE DISTANCE BETWEEN ANY TWO PEAKS OR VALLEYS IS CALLED WAVELENGTH.
WAVELENGTH
PEAK
VALLEY
JUST LIKE WAVES IN THE SEA

PROPERTIES OF LIGHT

LIGHT CAN TRAVEL IN VACUUM. THAT'S WHY WE SEE DISTANT OBJECTS LIKE SUN AND STARS AND RECEIVE LIGHT FROM THEM.

LIGHT HAS DIFFERENT PROPERTIES.

LIGHT TRAVELS IN A STRAIGHT LINE UNLESS ITS PATH IS OBSTRUCTED BY SOMETHING.

LIGHT IS THE FASTEST FORM OF ENERGY. IT TRAVELS AT A SPEED OF 186,000 MILES (300,000 KILOMETRES) PER SECOND.

LIGHT CAN TRAVEL IN ALL MEDIUMS

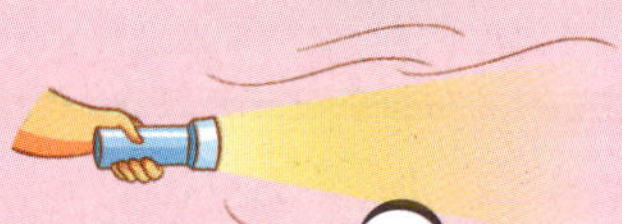

AIR

SOLID

LIQUID

VACUUM

BEHAVIOR OF LIGHT

LIGHT BEHAVES DIFFERENTLY WHEN IT HITS DIFFERENT KINDS OF OBJECTS.

REFLECTION

WHEN LIGHT HITS A SMOOTH OR SHINY SURFACE, IT BOUNCES OFF OR REFLECTS.

REFRACTION

LIGHT WAVES BEND WHEN THEY TRAVEL FROM ONE MEDIUM TO ANOTHER.

THIS HAPPENS BECAUSE ITS SPEED CHANGES AS IT TRAVELS THROUGH DIFFERENT MEDIUMS.

ABSORPTION

SOMETIMES, LIGHT DOES NOT BOUNCE OFF AN OBJECT OR PASS THROUGH IT. IN THAT CASE, IT IS ABSORBED BY THE OBJECT AND REMAINS IN IT AS ANOTHER FORM OF ENERGY.

A RAY OF WHITE LIGHT CAN BE SPLIT INTO ITS CONSTITUENT COLORS. THIS IS CALLED DISPERSION.

LIGHT CAN BE DISPERSED BY PASSING IT THROUGH A GLASS PRISM.

SUN

NATURAL SOURCES OF LIGHT

STARS

SOURCES OF LIGHT

A LIGHT SOURCE IS SOMETHING THAT RELEASES LIGHT FROM ITSELF. WE GET LIGHT FROM DIFFERENT SOURCES. THESE CAN BE NATURAL OR ARTIFICIAL.

FIRE

ARTIFICIAL SOURCES OF LIGHT

CANDLE

BULB

LASER

WE CAN CONTROL THE PROPERTIES OF LIGHT OBTAINED FROM ARTIFICIAL SOURCES SUCH AS INTENSITY, BRIGHTNESS, CONTRAST, ETC., UP TO A CERTAIN LEVEL BUT WE CANNOT CONTROL THE NATURAL SOURCES OF LIGHT.

GLOW STICK

SUNLIGHT
THE SUN IS THE SOURCE OF NATURAL LIGHT AND ALL ENERGY ON EARTH.
DO YOU KNOW HOW SUNLIGHT IS PRODUCED?
THE SUN PRODUCES LIGHT WHEN HYDROGEN ATOMS INSIDE IT FUSE TOGETHER AND MAKE HELIUM.
THIS PROCESS CREATES HUGE AMOUNTS OF ENERGY IN THE FORM OF HEAT, LIGHT AND RADIATION WHICH SPREADS IN ALL DIRECTIONS INTO SPACE.
SOME OF THIS LIGHT TRAVELS TO EARTH, WHICH WE CALL SUNLIGHT.
SUNLIGHT IS ALSO CALLED VISIBLE LIGHT. ALONG WITH THE VISIBLE LIGHT, THE SUN ALSO EMITS ULTRAVIOLET RAYS WHICH WE CANNOT SEE.

PLANTS NEED SUNLIGHT TO GROW.
ANIMALS AND HUMANS ARE DEPENDENT ON PLANTS FOR FOOD AND OXYGEN.
NEED OF SUNLIGHT
THE EARTH WOULD BE A COLD AND LIFELESS PLANET WITHOUT SUNLIGHT.
WITHOUT SUNLIGHT, THERE WOULD BE NO WINDS, CLOUDS OR OCEAN CURRENTS.
IT TAKES 8 MINUTES AND 20 SECONDS FOR SUNLIGHT TO REACH EARTH.

LUMINOUS AND NON-LUMINOUS OBJECTS
SUN
STARS
OBJECTS THAT CAN EMIT LIGHT OF THEIR OWN ARE CALLED LUMINOUS OBJECTS.
LUMINOUS OBJECTS
FIREFLIES
BULB
NON-LUMINOUS OBJECTS
OBJECTS THAT CANNOT EMIT LIGHT OF THEIR OWN ARE CALLED NON-LUMINOUS OBJECTS.
TABLE
NOTEBOOK
WE CAN SEE NON-LUMINOUS OBJECTS BECAUSE THEY REFLECT LIGHT FROM OTHER SOURCES.
TREE
MOON

LIGHT AND SIGHT

SIGHT IS ONE OF THE FIVE SENSES. EYES ARE THE ORGANS OF SIGHT. WE GET MOST OF THE INFORMATION ABOUT THE WORLD AROUND US THROUGH OUR EYES.

HOW LIGHT HELPS US TO SEE OBJECTS?

WHEN WE SEE THINGS AROUND US, WE ACTUALLY SEE THE LIGHT THAT BOUNCES OFF THEM. LIGHT IS REFLECTED FROM OBJECTS AND ENTERS OUR EYES.

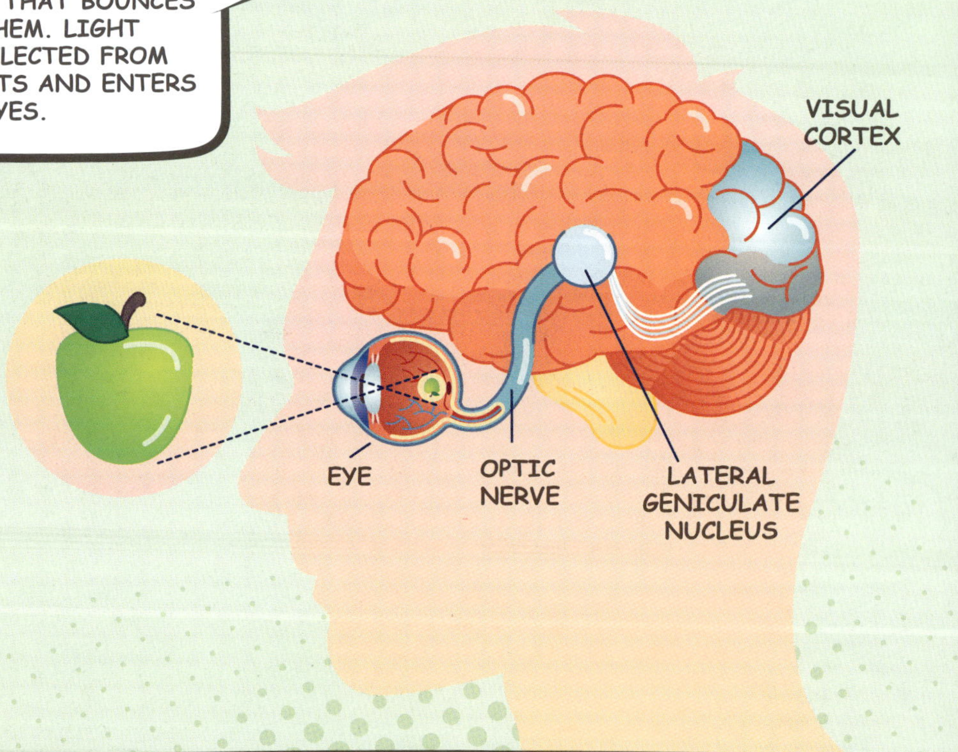

OUR EYES TRANSFORM LIGHT INTO SIGNALS THAT OUR BRAIN CAN UNDERSTAND. THE BRAIN TURNS THEM INTO IMAGES WHICH WE CAN SEE.

THE HUMAN EYE

CORNEA

LIGHT ENTERS THE EYES THROUGH THE CORNEA. IT IS A CLEAR, DOME-SHAPED PROTECTIVE LAYER IN FRONT OF OUR EYES.

PUPIL

LIGHT THEN TRAVELS THROUGH PUPIL INTO THE EYE. IT CONTROLS THE AMOUNT OF LIGHT ENTERING OUR EYES.

BLOOD VESSELS

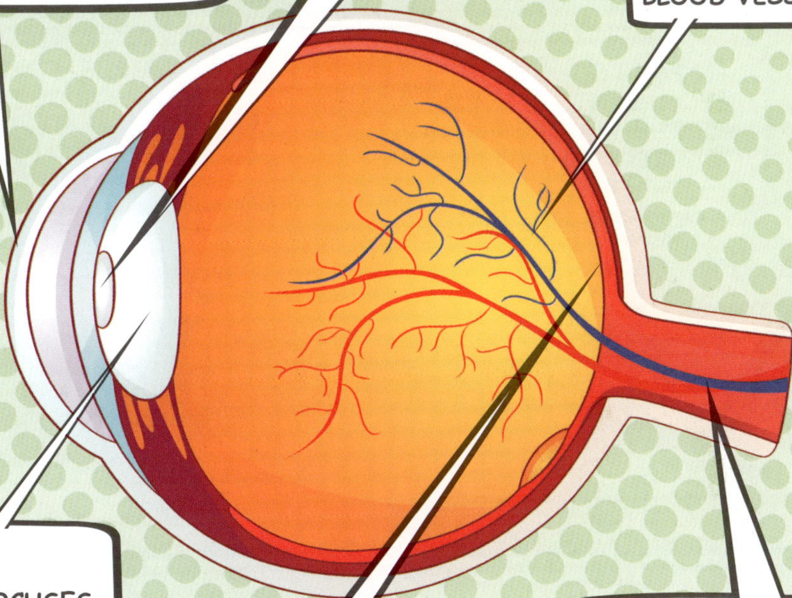

LENS

THE LENS FOCUSES LIGHT RAYS ON THE RETINA.

OPTIC NERVE

THE OPTIC NERVE SENDS THE INFORMATION TO THE BRAIN IN THE FORM OF ELECTRICAL SIGNALS.

RETINA

THE LIGHT LANDS ON THE RETINA! AN UPSIDE-DOWN IMAGE OF THE OBJECT IS FORMED ON IT.

THE RETINA THEN TRANSFERS THE INFORMATION TO THE OPTIC NERVE.

THE BRAIN TURNS THE IMAGE THE RIGHT WAY UP AND WE SEE THE OBJECT.

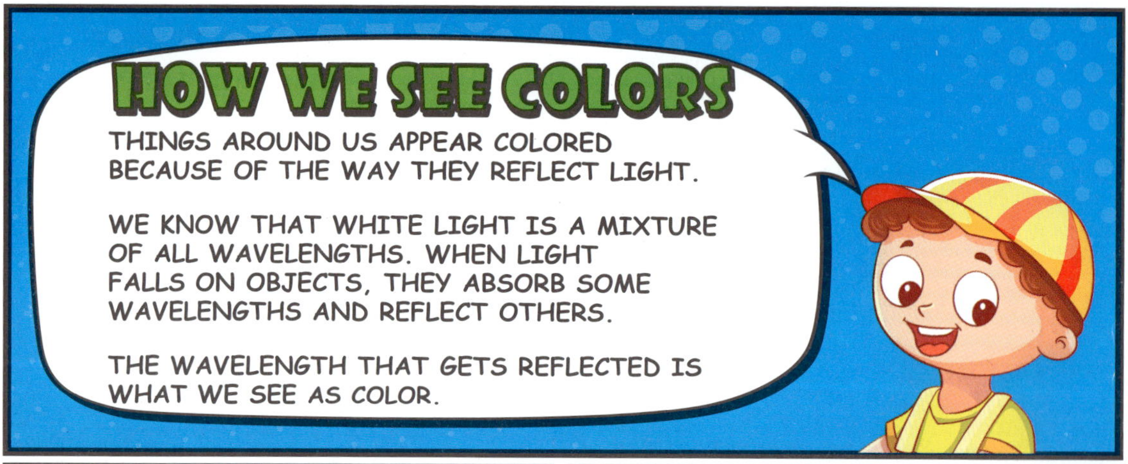

IS THE SKY REALLY BLUE?

WHILE TRAVELING TO EARTH, WHEN SUNLIGHT ENTERS THE ATMOSPHERE, IT IS SCATTERED IN ALL DIRECTIONS BY THE GASES AND PARTICLES PRESENT IN AIR.

BLUE LIGHT IS SCATTERED MORE THAN THE OTHER COLORS OF SUNLIGHT. WHEN WE LOOK UP, WE ACTUALLY SEE THE BLUE LIGHT SCATTERED ALL OVER, WHICH MAKES THE SKY APPEAR BLUE.

TRANSPARENT, TRANSLUCENT AND OPAQUE OBJECTS

DIFFERENT OBJECTS INTERACT WITH LIGHT IN DIFFERENT WAYS WHEN LIGHT HITS THEM. SOME OBJECTS ALLOW LIGHT TO PASS THROUGH THEM AND SOME DON'T.

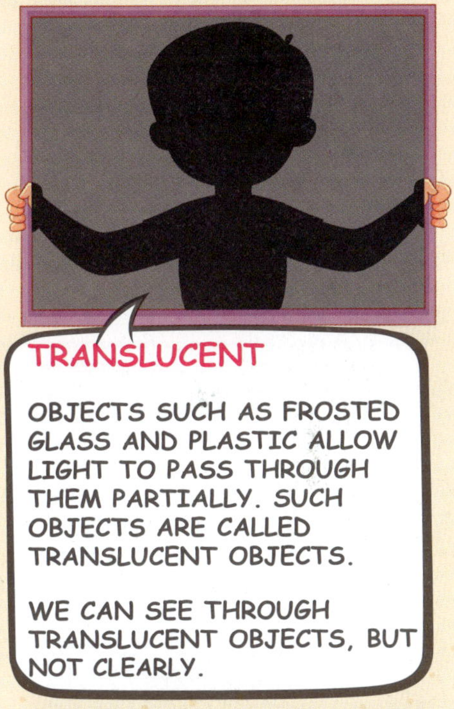

TRANSPARENT

OBJECTS SUCH AS GLASS THAT ALLOW LIGHT TO PASS THROUGH THEM COMPLETELY ARE CALLED TRANSPARENT OBJECTS.

WE CAN SEE CLEARLY THROUGH TRANSPARENT OBJECTS.

TRANSLUCENT

OBJECTS SUCH AS FROSTED GLASS AND PLASTIC ALLOW LIGHT TO PASS THROUGH THEM PARTIALLY. SUCH OBJECTS ARE CALLED TRANSLUCENT OBJECTS.

WE CAN SEE THROUGH TRANSLUCENT OBJECTS, BUT NOT CLEARLY.

OPAQUE

OBJECTS SUCH AS WOOD AND METAL DO NOT ALLOW LIGHT TO PASS THROUGH THEM. SUCH OBJECTS ARE CALLED OPAQUE OBJECTS.

WE CANNOT SEE THROUGH OPAQUE OBJECTS AT ALL.

SHADOWS
A SHADOW IS A DARK AREA FORMED WHEN SOMETHING BLOCKS THE WAY OF LIGHT.
LIGHT TRAVELS IN STRAIGHT LINES FROM A SOURCE.
WHEN AN OPAQUE OBJECT COMES IN THE PATH OF LIGHT, IT STOPS LIGHT RAYS FROM PASSING THROUGH IT.
AS A RESULT, A DARK AREA IS FORMED BEHIND THE OBJECT. THIS IS CALLED SHADOW.
SHADOW
OPAQUE OBJECT
THE SHAPE AND SIZE OF THE SHADOW DEPENDS ON THE POSITION AND SIZE OF THE LIGHT SOURCE.
THE SUN IS IN LOW HORIZON IN THE MORNING AND EVENING.
THE SHADOW FORMED DURING THIS TIME IS LONGER AND BLURRED.
THE SUN IS HIGH IN THE SKY AT NOON.
THE SHADOW FORMED IS SHORT AND DARK.

REFLECTION OF LIGHT

SIMILARLY, WHEN LIGHT HITS A SURFACE, IT BOUNCES OFF AND CHANGES DIRECTION. THIS IS CALLED **REFLECTION OF LIGHT**.

THIS IS HOW REFLECTION OCCURS:

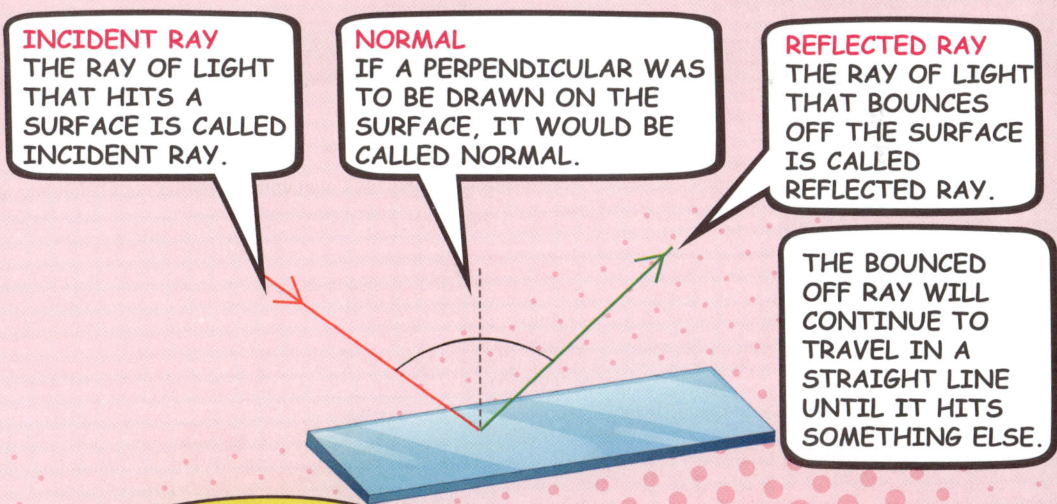

TYPES OF REFLECTION

LIGHT IS REFLECTED IN TWO WAYS.

SPECULAR REFLECTION

WHEN LIGHT HITS A SMOOTH SURFACE SUCH AS A PLANE MIRROR, IT IS REFLECTED AT A DEFINITE ANGLE. SUCH A REFLECTION IS CALLED SPECULAR OR REGULAR REFLECTION.

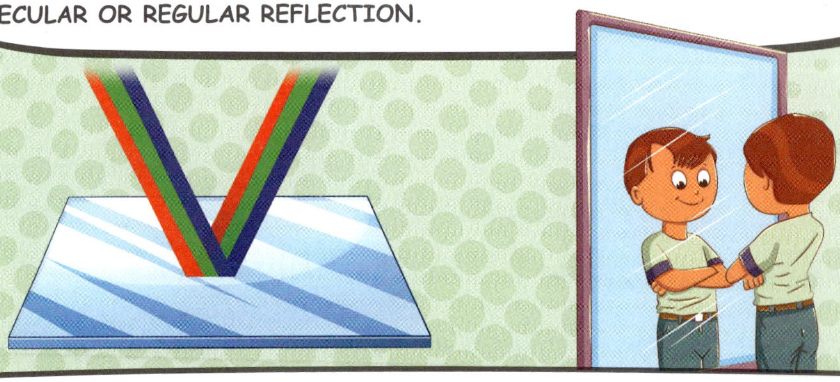

A REGULAR REFLECTION RESULTS IN THE FORMATION OF A SHARP IMAGE. THIS IS BECAUSE ALL THE LIGHT THAT FALLS ON THE SURFACE IS REFLECTED UNIFORMLY.

DIFFUSE REFLECTION

WHEN LIGHT HITS UNEVEN AND ROUGH SURFACES, IT IS REFLECTED AT DIFFERENT ANGLES AND GETS SCATTERED IN ALL DIRECTIONS. SUCH A REFLECTION IS CALLED DIFFUSE OR IRREGULAR REFLECTION.

THE IMAGE FORMED BY DIFFUSE REFLECTION IS BLURRED. THIS IS BECAUSE LIGHT THAT FALLS ON AN UNEVEN SURFACE IS REFLECTED IN COMPLETELY DIFFERENT DIRECTIONS.

REFRACTION OF LIGHT

PUT A PENCIL IN A CLEAR GLASS OF WATER. OBSERVE HOW IT LOOKS. WHY DON'T THE TOP AND BOTTOM OF THE PENCIL SEEM TO FIT TOGETHER?

IT IS DUE TO THE **REFRACTION OF LIGHT**.

REFRACTION IS A PHENOMENON IN WHICH LIGHT RAYS BEND WHEN THEY TRAVEL FROM ONE MEDIUM TO ANOTHER.

THIS HAPPENS BECAUSE LIGHT TRAVELS AT DIFFERENT SPEEDS IN DIFFERENT MEDIUMS.

REFRACTION OF LIGHT IN WATER

REFRACTION OF LIGHT IN AIR

REFLECTION AND REFRACTION IN DAILY LIFE

THE FOLLOWING HAPPENS DUE TO THE REFLECTION OF LIGHT:

THE FOLLOWING HAPPENS DUE TO THE REFRACTION OF LIGHT:
A RAINBOW IS FORMED
STARS TWINKLE
PEOPLE CAN CORRECT THEIR VISION USING SPECTACLES
WE CAN TAKE PICTURES USING A CAMERA
MIRAGES ARE FORMED
REFLECTION AND REFRACTION WORK TOGETHER
A MICROSCOPE HELPS US TO EXAMINE OBJECTS THAT CANNOT BE SEEN BY THE NAKED EYE
WE CAN LOOK INTO SPACE USING A TELESCOPE

MIRRORS AND IMAGES

A MIRROR IS A SMOOTH, FLAT SURFACE THAT SHOWS REFLECTION OF OBJECTS NEAR IT.

MIRRORS ARE MOSTLY MADE OF GLASS, COATED WITH A SHINY METAL ON THE BACK.

THE IMAGE OF AN OBJECT FORMED IN THE MIRROR IS CALLED ITS REFLECTION.

MIRRORS ARE OF DIFFERENT KINDS.

PLANE MIRRORS
PLANE MIRRORS ARE FLAT. THEY SHOW A REVERSED IMAGE.

SPHERICAL MIRRORS
SPHERICAL MIRRORS HAVE CURVED OR SPHERICAL REFLECTING SURFACES. THERE ARE TWO KINDS OF SPHERICAL MIRRORS-CONVEX AND CONCAVE.

CONVEX MIRRORS

CONVEX MIRRORS ARE CURVED ON THE OUTSIDE. THEY MAKE OBJECTS LOOK UPRIGHT AND SMALLER THAN THEY REALLY ARE.

CONCAVE MIRRORS

CONCAVE MIRRORS ARE CURVED ON THE INSIDE, LIKE A BOWL. THEY MAKE OBJECTS LOOK NEARER AND BIGGER THAN THEY REALLY ARE.

HOWEVER, WHEN OBJECTS ARE CLOSE TO A CONVEX MIRROR, THEY APPEAR LARGER THAN THEIR ACTUAL SIZE.